Bygone Ba...

A POSTCARD TOUR OF RUSTIC NEW ENGLAND

BY EARL BRECHLIN

DOWN EAST BOOKS · CAMDEN, MAINE · WWW.DOWNEASTBOOKS.COM

To Baba: your spirit still fills so many of these places.

ISBN: 0-89272-636-9
LCCN: 2004117296
DESIGN BY LURELLE CHEVERIE
PRINTED IN CHINA. RPS

2 4 5 3 1

DOWN EAST BOOKS
A DIVISION OF DOWN EAST ENTERPRISE, INC.
PUBLISHER OF *DOWN EAST*, THE MAGAZINE OF MAINE

BOOK ORDERS: 1-800-685-7962
WWW.DOWNEASTBOOKS.COM

ON THE COVER: THIS ARTIST'S RENDERING OF A MAINE BULL MOOSE ILLUMINATED BY A FULL MOON EPITOMIZES THE VICTORIAN NOTION THAT WILD BEASTS LURKED EVERYWHERE IN THE BACKWOODS OF NEW ENGLAND.

ALL POSTCARDS FROM THE AUTHOR'S COLLECTION UNLESS OTHERWISE NOTED.

Preface Despite the fact that the North American continent, particularly the East Coast, had long been settled, Americans at the turn of the twentieth century seemed reluctant to cast aside the notion that there was no longer a limitless wild and untamed country just outside their doors. The backwoods were still seen as a place in need of subjugation, improvement, civilization—an imperfect landscape awaiting the artificial stamp of man, if you will. Yet electric lights, the telephone, the internal combustion engine, and a rapidly growing fleet of private cars were making the world a much, much smaller place.

Increased mobility and leisure time resulted in the advent of vacations for the middle class, with people exploring and visiting natural wonders and man-made sights that were formerly unreachable by all save those willing to endure several days of arduous travel. In hopes of attracting tourists, nearly every town rushed to spread the word about unique geological features. When true natural wonders were in short supply, promoters used their imaginations to name and exhibit unusual rock formations that, when viewed from just the right angle, looked like some fanciful creature, historic figure, or domestic animal.

It seemed as though every town in New England could lay claim to having at least one outcropping of rock that, sometimes with some not-so-subtle help from sledgehammers or dynamite, bore an uncanny resemblance to Martha Washington. Grand hotels, railroads to the clouds, mountaintop inns, sporting camps, and quaint villages became "natural" destinations unto themselves.

Communities across the region rushed to build imposing war memorials or observation towers. Tens of thousands of people on the interstate highways today drive by some of these edifices daily; few know anything about them.

Without radio or television at the turn of the twentieth century, or even easy-to-use personal cameras, postcards were the popular way for promoters to advertise and for tourists to document a trip and share the adventure with the folks back home.

Today, collecting antique postcards is a comparatively inexpensive way to preserve a piece of that innocent past. The affection they engender creates a bond to bygone days in much the same way that the history of these special places continues to capture our hearts today. In some respects, the glimpse of days gone by provided by old postcards allows people of this time to take a trip not only to a place they may know well or one day hope to visit but to a place where no one can ever hope to go—another time. 🖎

1. The tradition of Maine sporting camps goes back more than 150 years. Typically the camps are located on lakes or rivers with individual guest cabins and a central lodge for meals. Even today, the cabins often have no electricity and are heated only with wood. These bastions of civilization in the state's untamed places attract not only hunters and fishermen but also hikers, canoeists, artists, writers, and those who just want to escape the teeming cities or the humdrum of everyday life. In 1904 there were an estimated three hundred sporting camps in Maine. By 1997 there were only seventy-eight. Most are now members of the Maine Sporting Camps Association. Tim Pond Camps in Eustis bills itself as the oldest continuously operated sporting camp in New England.

A Maine Sporting Camp.

2. Sleeping out under the stars in the North Woods of Maine conjures up a romantic image of a crackling fire with a canopy of bright stars. Early adventurers endured canvas tents, bulky blankets, and heavy cast iron pots and pans. Modern campers enjoy light, warm, easy-to-maintain gear. Maine provides that experience at hundreds of private campgrounds and at tenting facilities in 12 of the state's 32 state parks. For those wishing a more backcountry experience, there are hundreds of sites in Maine's North Woods, along the Allagash Wilderness Waterway, in roadless areas in Baxter State Park, or along the nearly 267 miles of the Appalachian Trail in Maine.

CAMPING IN THE MAINE WOODS

112035

3. THE TOTAL LENGTH OF MAINE'S APPROXIMATELY
7,000 RIVERS, STREAMS, AND BROOKS COMES TO JUST
UNDER 34,000 MILES. BROOKS ACCOUNT FOR ABOUT
23,000 MILES OF THAT. PERHAPS BECAUSE OF MAINE'S
SIZE, ITS PLACE NAMES ARE OFTEN DUPLICATED. THE
STATE HAS THIRTY-SEVEN BOG BROOKS, TWENTY-FIVE
BEAVER BROOKS, TWENTY-THREE ALDER BROOKS, AND,
FOR THE ANGLERS OUT THERE, EIGHTEEN TROUT BROOKS.
THE LONGEST RIVER IN MAINE, THE PENOBSCOT, EXTENDS
SOME 240 MILES AND DRAINS MORE THAN 8,000 SQUARE
MILES. IT DUMPS, ON AVERAGE, MORE THAN 10 BILLION
GALLONS OF WATER A DAY INTO PENOBSCOT BAY.

A Maine trout Stream.

4. LUMBERJACKS WORKED ALL WINTER IN THE MAINE WOODS AND STOCKPILED PULPWOOD AND SAWLOGS FOR THE ANNUAL SPRING RUN DOWNSTREAM TO MILLS. AN ESTIMATED 150 MILLION LOGS WERE MOVED BY WATER ANNUALLY. HUNDREDS OF DAMS ENSURED CONTROL OF THE WATER. RIVER DRIVING WAS TOUGH, DANGEROUS WORK, ESPECIALLY WHEN LOGS JAMMED AT RAPIDS OR NARROW SPOTS. IF THE KEY LOG COULD NOT BE FOUND AND COAXED LOOSE, DYNAMITE HAD TO BE USED.

In The Maine Woods,
Log Driving.

67683 W

5. Life in the earliest logging camps in the mid-1800s was primitive, to say the least. Rough structures made of logs were used for both sleeping and eating. Fires were kindled in the middle of the building, with openings in the roof for the smoke. On the low side a single platform bed ran the whole length, often with tree boughs or other vegetation for cushioning. A dozen or more men, who went for months without bathing, slept side by side in their long johns under a single long blanket. They worked fourteen-hour days cutting down trees and sawing them up by hand. The cook kept them fortified with four meals a day—breakfast, two lunches, and supper. Oxen were usually sheltered in a roofed-over pen.

A Maine Logging Camp.

6. LUMBERJACKS WORKING LONG HOURS IN THE MAINE OUT-
DOORS, PARTICULARLY IN WINTER, NEEDED A LOT OF FOOD TO
KEEP THEM GOING. A GOOD COOK WAS WORTH HIS WEIGHT IN
GOLD. ONE STAPLE, ADOPTED FROM THE PENOBSCOT INDIANS,
WAS BAKED BEANS COOKED IN A HOLE IN THE GROUND. A
ROARING FIRE WAS NURTURED FOR HALF A DAY OR MORE IN A
STONE-LINED PIT. THE DRIED BEANS, MIXED WITH MOLASSES,
WATER, AND A LIBERAL HELPING OF SALT PORK, WERE PLACED
IN A CAST-IRON POT WITH A STURDY LID AND LOWERED INTO
THE HOLE. COVERED WITH EMBERS AND A LAYER OF SOIL, THE
POT OF BEANS WAS LEFT TO SIMMER FOR SIXTEEN HOURS.
MANY A LOGGER ENJOYED BEANS AT EVERY MEAL, INCLUDING
BREAKFAST. BEAN HOLE BEANS REMAIN A POPULAR STAPLE
OF PUBLIC SUPPERS TODAY.

A Maine Logging Camp. The Cook at the "Bean-hole"

7. CANOES OR WOODEN DORIES CALLED BATEAUX WERE THE PREFERRED METHOD OF LONG-DISTANCE TRAVEL THROUGH MAINE'S NEARLY IMPASSABLE FORESTS DURING THE EARLY YEARS OF EUROPEAN SETTLEMENT. TODAY, MAINE RESIDENTS OWN MORE THAN 150,000 CANOES AND KAYAKS AND TAKE GREAT PLEASURE IN EXPLORING RUSHING RIVERS AND QUIET BACKCOUNTRY BOGS AND PONDS. THE OLD TOWN CANOE COMPANY WAS ESTABLISHED IN 1900, AND BY 1910 IT WAS SELLING 3,500 WOOD-AND-CANVAS CANOES ANNUALLY. THE COMPANY CELE-BRATED PRODUCTION OF ITS ONE MILLIONTH BOAT IN 2003. IT IS THE LARGEST CANOE MANUFACTURER IN THE WORLD.

In the Maine Woods.

8. Located at the southeast end of Kennebago Lake, the Lake House was one of a series of camps and guesthouses created on that spot. As of 1912 the property included a ten-room main lodge and thirteen cabins. Electricity was installed four years later. During World War II the establishment was closed. It reopened after the war and was expanded and renovated, but its fortunes waned. The furnishings were sold off in 1972, and the main building was torn down in 1974.

548 KENNEBAGO LAKE HOUSE AND CAMP, MAINE

You might write twice in a while I think. J.M.C.

9. Upper Dam, which separates Upper Richardson Lake from Mooselookmeguntic Lake, is the official starting place of the Androscoggin River. The Upper Dam House operated from the late 1800s until the early 1950s. Resident Carrie Stevens, the wife of a local guide, created one of fly-fishing's most famous flies, the Grey Ghost Streamer. Supposedly on her first cast with this fly into the pool below the dam, she landed a six-pound trout.

Built to facilitate logging operations, the early dams in the Rangeley Lakes area were of traditional timber, rock, and earth construction. Middle Dam, which is fifteen hundred feet long, raised the level of the lake nine feet.

Lake Mooselookmeguntic, Me.,
Upper Dam House and Cottages.

10. LOCATED ON THE NORTH SHORE OF RANGELEY LAKE NEAR THE OUTLET, THE MOUNTAIN VIEW HOUSE BEGAN AS A MODEST CAMP BUILT BY GEORGE SOULE IN 1873. VARIOUS BUILDINGS WERE ADDED OR REMOVED OVER THE YEARS. BY 1900 THE GRAND ESTABLISHMENT COULD ACCOMMODATE EIGHTY-FIVE GUESTS AND FEATURED A FIREPLACE THAT COULD ACCEPT FIVE-FOOT LOGS. AS WITH MANY OF MAINE'S GRAND SPORTING HOTELS, THIS ONE'S FORTUNES FADED AFTER IT WAS CLOSED DURING WORLD WAR II. THE MAIN BUILDING WAS DEMOLISHED IN 1952. THE ANNEX, CONTAINING A DINING ROOM AND A COCKTAIL LOUNGE, BURNED IN 1956. THE PROPERTY WAS SOLD OFF AS PRIVATE LOTS IN THE EARLY 1960S.

Mountain View House,   Rangeley Lake, Me.

11. In the early years of freshwater fishing in Maine, there were no catch limits. Some fishermen boasted of catching as many as two hundred trout in a day. Today, regulations governing catch limits and tackle seem to differ for every lake or river. Catch and release is a popular approach. Maine is fortunate to have lakes that are ideal habitat for cold-water species such as brown trout, lake trout (togue), brook trout, rainbow trout, and landlocked salmon, as well as ponds ideally suited for warm-water species such as large- and smallmouth bass, perch, and northern pike. Officials estimate that as many as 380,000 people fish in Maine annually. They generate more than $84 million for the economy.

A Morning Catch.

12. The first building of what would become the Rangeley Hotel was built in 1877 on the spot where the Rangeley Inn is today. In 1895 the building was cut in two and moved at great cost to the eastern shore of Rangeley Lake. The business grew over the years until the establishment boasted nearly 70 rooms and a dining room that could seat 350. The property was renamed the Rangeley Lake Hotel after Charles Day took it over in 1928. Mr. Day had crews remove the many rocks between the lake and the hotel and create formal gardens. The installation of an elevator and electric lights only increased the hotel's popularity. Its fortunes waned after World War II, however. In the late 1950s the furnishings were sold off, the buildings were razed, and the property was subdivided.

Rangeley Hotel, Rangeley Lake, Me.

13. THE RANGELEY LAKES REGION WAS ONE OF THE FIRST AREAS IN MAINE TO BEGIN ATTRACTING SCORES OF VISITORS. THEY STARTED COMING IN THE LATE 1800s, LURED BY STORIES OF COOL SUMMERS AND LAKES TEEMING WITH FISH. MAINE HAS 5,785 BODIES OF WATER GREATER THAN ONE ACRE IN SIZE. "GREAT PONDS"—THOSE OF MORE THAN TEN ACRES—ARE CONSIDERED TO BE PUBLIC PROPERTY. MAINE HAS MORE THAN 2,600.

BALD MOUNTAIN CAMPS WAS FOUNDED IN 1897 ON THE EASTERN SIDE OF MOOSELOOKMEGUNTIC LAKE. THE VIEW ON THE CARD SHOWS "SPORTS" ON THEIR PORCHES AROUND 1900. ALTHOUGH SEVERAL CABINS WERE DESTROYED BY FIRE IN 1914, BALD MOUNTAIN CAMPS GREW OVER THE YEARS, AND BY 1955 THERE WERE FIFTEEN CABINS. THE CAMPS ARE STILL IN OPERATION TODAY.

Rangeley Lakes, Me, Bald Mountain Camps

14. ALTHOUGH THE FIRST MILLS AT RUMFORD TO BE POWERED BY THE ANDROSCOGGIN RIVER IN THE MID-1800S WERE SIMPLE GRISTMILLS AND SAWMILLS WITH MODEST SPILLWAYS, HEAVY INDUSTRY WAS SOON TO FOLLOW. ATTRACTED BY A RIVER THAT DROPPED 177 FEET IN A MILE OVER A SERIES OF CASCADES, PAPER MILLS AND ELECTRICITY PRODUCERS RUSHED TO BUILD PLANTS. IN FACT, RUMFORD FALLS HAS THE HIGHEST VOLUME OF WATER OVER ANY FALLS EAST OF NIAGARA. OXFORD PAPER COMPANY, WHICH OPENED ITS MILL IN 1893, AT ONE TIME WAS THE LARGEST PAPER PRODUCER UNDER ONE ROOF IN THE WORLD. RUMFORD CAN ALSO LAY CLAIM TO BEING THE BIRTHPLACE OF U.S. SENATOR EDMUND MUSKIE, WHO ALSO SERVED AS MAINE'S GOVERNOR AND THE COUNTRY'S SECRETARY OF STATE.

DAM AT POWER STATION, ANDROSCOGGIN RIVER, RUMFORD, MAINE.   93877

15. Maine once boasted more than 120 covered bridges. They were practical—the sides and roof kept rain and snow off the supporting timbers. Over the years most of these bridges have succumbed to fire, flood, or ice; only nine remain. More photographs and paintings have been done of the Artist's Bridge, over Sunday River in Newry, than any of the others. This 87-foot-long bridge, a Paddleford truss design, was built in 1872. The bridge was closed to vehicular traffic in 1958.

Bethel, Me., Artists Bridge.

Very rough weather with us
H. 11. 07 Mrs. L. Sharetts

16. Made entirely of logs, the Moosehorn Cabin was constructed in the 1800s as one of the Dexter area's earliest recreational clubs. Local businessmen used the facility for fishing, snowshoeing, and get-togethers on the shore of 1,062-acre Wassookeag Lake. The cabin was torn down in the early 1900s so the land could be used as a youth summer camp. According to local lore, *Wassookeag* is the Penobscot Indian word for "shining lake."

Dexter, Me.   Moosehorn Cabin.

17. FROM HUMBLE BEGINNINGS AS A STAGECOACH STOP IN THE LATE 1700s, THE POLAND SPRING HOUSE GREW STEADILY, BUOYED BY THE REPUTATION OF THE HEALING POWERS OF A NEARBY SPRING FOUND IN 1844. THE HOTEL EVENTUALLY GREW TO THREE HUNDRED ROOMS. IT WAS A FAVORITE HAUNT OF CELEBRITIES AND PRESIDENTS AND WAS BOOKED YEARS IN ADVANCE. THE STEADY STREAM OF VISITORS CAME VIA RAIL THROUGH THE STATION AT NEARBY DANVILLE JUNCTION. MUHAMMAD ALI, THEN KNOWN AS CASSIUS CLAY, TRAINED AT THE HOTEL BEFORE HIS FIGHT WITH SONNY LISTON IN 1972. THE GRAND WOOD-FRAMED BUILDING BURNED DOWN IN 1975.

POLAND SPRING WATER GREW IN REPUTATION ALONG WITH THE RESORT. THE POLAND SPRING COMPANY NOW PUMPS AND SELLS 400 MILLION GALLONS OF WATER A YEAR FROM THE SAME AQUIFER THAT FEEDS THE SPRING.

POLAND SPRING HOUSE, SOUTH POLAND, ME.

18. RUNNING STRAIGHT THROUGH THE HEART OF MAINE FROM NEW BRUNSWICK IN THE EAST TO QUEBEC IN THE WEST, THE CANADIAN PACIFIC RAILROAD TRAVERSES SOME OF THE WILDEST AND MOST SCENIC AREAS OF THE STATE. REMOTE ONAWA TRESTLE, OVER SHIP POND STREAM, IS THE HIGHEST RAILROAD BRIDGE IN MAINE, AT 130 FEET. THE BRIDGE SHOWN IN THIS VIEW WAS REPLACED IN 1931. THE HANDFUL OF CAMPS IN THE VILLAGE OF ONAWA AT ONE TIME WAS REACHABLE ONLY BY RAILROAD. IN THE BACKGROUND IS 2,000-FOOT BORESTONE MOUNTAIN, WHICH IS HOME TO A HIKING AND NATURE PRESERVE OWNED BY THE MAINE AUDUBON SOCIETY.

C. P. R. R. Trestle, Onawa, Me.

19. THE GAME POLE OUTSIDE THIS CAMP HANGS HEAVY WITH FOUR WHITE-TAILED DEER. DEER LIKE TO LIVE IN FRINGE AREAS BETWEEN FIELDS AND WOODS. IN FACT, BECAUSE OF HUMAN LAND CLEARING THERE ARE MORE DEER IN MAINE TODAY THAN WHEN THE PILGRIMS LANDED AT PLYMOUTH ROCK. EACH FALL MORE THAN 164,000 HUNTERS TAKE TO MAINE'S WOODS FOR THE MONTH-LONG OPEN SEASON. THE DEER POPULATION IN MAINE IS NOW ESTIMATED TO BE AROUND 250,000 ANIMALS, WITH THE HIGHEST CONCENTRATION BEING IN WALDO COUNTY. WILDLIFE OFFICIALS HAVE ESTIMATED THE DENSITY THERE IN SOME YEARS AT 34 DEER PER SQUARE MILE.

Getting ready for Supper in a Typical Sporting Camp.

20. Moose are the Moosehead Lake region's claim to fame. These gangly creatures, which can weigh as much as 1,400 pounds when full grown, were hunted almost to extirpation in the early 1900s, when only an estimated 2,000 were left in the state. A ban on hunting from 1936 until 1979 helped the population rebound to today's nearly 30,000 animals. A moose eats as much as fifty to sixty pounds of vegetation in a day.

Considered to be the largest lake wholly contained in one state east of the Mississippi River, Moosehead is the headwaters of the mighty Kennebec River. The lake covers nearly 120 square miles and is 30 miles long and 10 miles wide.

Moose in Woods, Moosehead Lake, Me.

21. Built in 1889 for the then princely sum of $23,000, the fifty-seven-room Moosehead Inn was located at the south end of West Cove, where Currier's Flying Service is located today. Manager Henry Bartley reported to a large group of investors who wanted to ensure that guests got the top service promised for their two dollars a day. The building even had a wine room "for guests' goods." The inn burned down on March 5, 1912. Today, another establishment called the Moosehead Inn is located in Rockwood, on the west side of the lake north of Greenville Junction. Greenville, just down the road to the east, was first settled in 1824.

GREENVILLE JUNCTION, ME. MOOSEHEAD INN.

22. A. W. and W. I. Gerrish built a steam-powered sawmill on the east shore of West Cove in Greenville Junction in 1895. The logs processed by the mill were floated in large rafts down the lake with the assistance of steamboats. The rafts were corralled by long logs connected by lengths of chain. This view of the brothers' mill is circa 1906. Shortly afterward, the facility burned down.

Greenville Junction sported a large steamboat wharf, where passengers from the Bangor & Piscataquis Railroad and those from the Canadian Pacific Railroad could depart for trips to camps all along Moosehead Lake.

GREENVILLE JUNCTION, ME. GERRISH SAW MILL.

23. Still the grand lady of Moosehead Lake, the steamer *Katahdin* was built in 1914 by Bath Iron Works. The 104-foot-long steel vessel was once part of a fleet of nearly fifty steamboats that served the communities and sporting camps around the lake. Long ago converted to diesel power, the "Kate," as her fans call her, was used in the mid-twentieth century to tow booms of logs on the lake. She participated in the last log drive in 1975. Now maintained and operated daily by Greenville's Moosehead Marine Museum, which preserves the region's "steamy" past, the *Katahdin* is listed as a National Historic Landmark.

Steamer Katahdin on Moosehead Lake, Me.

24. THE FANCIFUL FLYING MACHINE (A SHAMELESS ALTERATION ADDED BY THE PRINTER OF THIS CARD) HOVERS NEAR THE LOWER REACHES OF MOUNT KINEO. NATIVE AMERICANS FREQUENTED KINEO, WHERE THEY QUARRIED FLINT FOR ARROWHEADS AND OTHER TOOLS. THE IMPOSING CLIFFS ON THE EAST SIDE OF THE MOUNTAIN TOWER EIGHT HUNDRED FEET OVER THE LAKE AND EXTEND ANOTHER HUNDRED FEET BELOW THE WATER.

SETTLEMENT OF THE AREA BEGAN IN 1827. A SERIES OF HOTELS SOON SPRANG UP ON THE SITE. VISITORS TRAVELED TO KINEO VIA STEAMBOAT FROM GREENVILLE JUNCTION, OR FROM ROCKWOOD, WHICH WAS SERVED BY THE SOMERSET RAILROAD (AND LATER MAINE CENTRAL). ROCKWOOD WAS NAMED FOR HIRAM ROCKWOOD PAGE, WHO DECIDED IN 1909 THAT "KINEO STATION" NEEDED A POST OFFICE. THE POST OFFICE, AND SUBSEQUENTLY THE TOWN, WERE NAMED FOR HIM.

Moosehead Lake, Me. Flying at Mt. Kineo

25. FIVE VERSIONS OF THE MOUNT KINEO HOTEL (ALSO CALLED THE KINEO HOTEL AND THE KINEO HOUSE) WERE BUILT OVER THE YEARS, BEGINNING IN 1844. THE FIFTH WAS BUILT IN 1884 AND WAS ADDED TO AND EXPANDED UNTIL THE MAIN HOTEL AND SURROUNDING BUILDINGS COULD ACCOMMODATE 500 GUESTS. THEY WERE SERVED BY A STAFF OF MORE THAN 400. THE DINING ROOM ALONE COULD SEAT 400 PEOPLE. BY WORLD WAR I, THE KINEO HOTEL WAS BILLED AS THE LARGEST AND MOST LUXURIOUS INLAND HOTEL IN THE UNITED STATES. RAIL SERVICE TO ROCKWOOD WAS DISCONTINUED IN 1933, AND THE HOTEL'S FORTUNES WANED. DEMOLITION OF THE MAIN BUILDING BEGAN IN 1938, BUT BEFORE IT COULD BE FINISHED, FIRE LEVELED THE REMAINDER OF THE STRUCTURE. THE FIREPLACE IN THIS VIEW WAS IN THE ANNEX BUILDING, WHICH WAS FINALLY TORN DOWN IN THE 1990S.

MOOSEHEAD LAKE, ME.   FIRE PLACE, KINEO HOUSE.

26. Cornelia "Fly Rod" Crosby became famous promoting Maine's North Woods via a newspaper column and appearances at sporting exhibitions. She was born in Phillips in 1854 and ended up at Rangeley, where she took up fly-fishing and eventually became so adept that she reportedly landed two hundred trout in one day. She holds the distinction of being the first woman in Maine to shoot a caribou, and in 1898 she shot the last one legally taken, a buck. The legislature granted her license number one when it created the Maine Guide licensing program in 1897. Crosby died in a nursing home in Lewiston in 1946 at the ripe old age of ninety-three.

The Famous "Fly Rod" landing a big one at Mt. Kineo, Moosehead Lake, Me.

27. With more than sixty Maine Guides on the payroll, the Mount Kineo House made sure its guests had the finest advice possible as they fished the waters of Moosehead Lake. The guides lived in special housing on the property and were mostly local men. Following complaints of poor service, the Maine legislature passed a law in 1897 requiring hunting guides to register. Just over three thousand signed up. There are nearly as many today. To become a Registered Maine Guide today, an applicant must pass a background check, written tests, and oral examinations and show proficiency in woodcraft, safety, and first aid. Over the years, guide licenses have been specialized into categories, including recreational, fishing, hunting, and white-water rafting and sea kayaking. Master Guides must be qualified in several areas.

Guides at Kineo House

28. Charles Nelson was a Maine Guide all his adult life. He was born in December 1886 "somewhere in the Moosehead region." Paddling from a standing position, Mr. Nelson apparently set the local record for the fastest time over a mile in a race off Mount Kineo. According to officials at the Moosehead Historical Society, the competition was most likely part of the regular sporting events and contests held to entertain guests at the palatial Kineo House. Mr. Nelson, who was a member of the Masonic Lodge in Greenville for sixty years, died in 1977 at the age of ninety.

CHAS. NELSON MAKING CANOE MILE RECORD ON MOOSEHEAD LAKE, ME.

29. Millinocket means "land of many islands." The town, built completely by the Great Northern Paper Company, was chartered in 1901. The speed with which the community sprang up helped earn it the nickname "Magic City." It quickly attracted hard-working immigrants to work in the mill and in the woods. Unlike the practice in mill towns in Massachusetts, the company did not operate retail businesses. Workers were paid in cash and were free to trade with whomever they wished. Great Northern leased land to workers who wanted to build homes. The company also built key civic structures, such as a hospital and library, and the Great Northern Hotel.

MILLINOCKET, ME.   KATAHDIN AVENUE, MT. KATAHDIN IN THE DISTANCE.

30. At 5,267 feet high, just 13 feet short of a mile, Katahdin (those in the know don't put a "Mount" in front of it, because the name means "greatest mountain") is the highest peak in Maine. Katahdin inspired Henry David Thoreau during an aborted summit attempt in the late 1800s. Impressed by the massive boulders and jagged, soaring clouds, he wrote that the tops of mountains "are among the unfinished parts of the globe, whither it is a slight insult to the gods to climb and pry into their secrets, and try their effect on our humanity. Only daring and insolent men, perchance, go there." The centerpiece of 204,733-acre Baxter State Park, Katahdin is also the northern terminus of the Appalachian Trail.

MT. KATAHDIN, MAINE.

100702

31. Even though Katahdin is nearly forty miles away from Screw Auger Falls, its name was used to help promote the falls, which are located on a brook that drains into the Pleasant River near the Appalachian Trail in the Katahdin Iron Works region. Still, the fifteen-foot main drop of the multiple cascades pales in comparison with the thirty-foot waterfalls in nearby Gulf Hagas, a narrow four-hundred-foot-deep chasm that has been called the Grand Canyon of New England. You will need to lace up your hiking boots to get to these wonders. There are no roads into the gulf, and a visit requires a round-trip hike of more than eight miles on rugged, slippery, and sometimes dangerous trails.

SCREW- AUGER FALLS, MT. KATAHDIN, ME.

32. Although the area along the West Branch of the Penobscot River was first settled in 1829, there were only farms in present-day Millinocket until a group of Maine businessmen decided to build a paper mill complex there and founded Great Northern Paper in 1899. When the structure was finished in 1900, it was the largest such mill in the world. The company opened its second mill in East Millinocket in 1907. The owners of the paper mill worked closely with local labor unions and avoided the sort of strife seen in the coal industry during this period.

MILLINOCKET, ME.   GREAT NORTHERN PAPER CO. MILL.

33. Northern Maine had few roads, so rail provided the easiest access in the late nineteenth century. Chartered in 1864, the Bangor & Aroostook Railroad laid track and purchased existing lines until it stretched from Searsport, on the coast, to the farthest reaches of Aroostook County. Its top sources of freight revenue were pulp, paper, and potatoes. The railroad's passenger division published its own magazine, *In the Maine Woods,* to promote hunting, fishing, tramping (hiking), and patronage of sporting camps. The following verse appeared in a 1934 edition of *In the Maine Woods.*

> To hell with all my worries
> They are negligible at best.
> I leave for Maine tomorrow
> Where my soul can take a rest.

Waiting for the Freight.

34. LAKEWOOD PARK, WHICH FEATURED THIS GRAND LODGE, GRACED THE EAST SHORE OF NICKERSON LAKE, NEAR HOULTON, AROUND THE TURN OF THE TWENTIETH CENTURY. INCORPORATED IN 1831, HOULTON WAS ONE OF THE TEN RICHEST TOWNS IN THE UNITED STATES DURING THE HEYDAY OF THE VICTORIAN LOGGING ERA. THE TOWN IS THE COUNTY SEAT, OR SHIRE TOWN, OF AROOSTOOK COUNTY, KNOWN IN MAINE SIMPLY AS "THE COUNTY." THE LARGEST COUNTY IN MAINE, IT COVERS A LAND AREA GREATER THAN THE STATES OF CONNECTICUT AND RHODE ISLAND COMBINED. *AROOSTOOK* IS A NATIVE AMERICAN WORD FOR "BEAUTIFUL RIVER."

"Lakewood", Houlton, Me.

35. Although this card depicts Grand Lake Stream, the canoes have the conventional double-end shape rather than the signature square stern of the renowned Grand Laker canoe, which was designed for handling the big waves on the nearly 15,000 acres of West Grand Lake. To be a true Grand Laker, a canoe must be twenty feet long and unusually wide, be made of wood with a canvas or fiberglass hull, have a square stern, and be built in Grand Lake Stream Plantation. The hefty canoes can come in handy when landing lake trout, which can weigh up to twenty pounds. The village of Grand Lake Stream, which takes its name from the river that flows from West Grand Lake into Big Lake, boasts the highest concentration of Registered Maine Guides anywhere in the state.

The Morning Start, Grand Lake Stream, Me.

36. Located along the Moose River, famous for its thirty-four-mile Bow Trip for canoeists, the town of Jackman was first settled in 1819. It is named for Captain James Jackman, who was among the first to live there. The Bow Trip starts and ends on Attean Pond with only a few portages. Numerous sporting camps catering to anglers, hunters, hikers, and paddlers have operated on the shores and the islands of Attean Pond. Just west of Jackman on the Canadian Pacific tracks is the ghost town of Holeb, a once bustling village now home to a few private cabins.

Jackman, Maine, Sport at Attean Lake.

we are all well hoping this
will find you the same
from James Smith

37. Native Americans were the first to take advantage of the relatively flat two-mile canoe carry route between the northern tip of Moosehead Lake, which is the headwaters of the Kennebec River system, and the West Branch of the Penobscot River. A canal suggested for the site in 1816 was never built; however, a railway that used oxen to haul a cart along wooden rails soon began carrying people and cargo over the route. The tracks burned in 1860, and a road was built to accommodate conventional wagons, such as the one shown here. Inns, camps, and storehouses soon sprang up along the road. Around 1900 a hundred-foot pier was built at the Moosehead end of the route to accommodate the many steamboats plying the lake. Henry David Thoreau took advantage of the carry on his first trip to Maine, in 1846.

No. East Carry, Me., Canoe Wagon
loaded for West Branch of Penobscot.

a V. G.
Sept. 5th

38. As the largest state east of the Mississippi River, Maine has always had a reputation for bigness. The makers of this card, featuring a gigantic potato on a Bangor & Aroostook flatcar, decided to have some fun with Maine's largest agricultural export. Scots-Irish immigrants brought potatoes to Maine in the mid-1700s. By 1930 there were 6,000 potato farmers, mostly in Aroostook County. That number dropped to fewer than 600 by 1997. Maine is the sixth-largest producer of spuds in the USA. It ships some 1.6 billion pounds annually.

Just an Aroostook Potato

39. AT 3,491 FEET, THE SUMMIT OF MOUNT GREYLOCK IS THE HIGHEST POINT IN THE STATE OF MASSACHUSETTS. ONCE CALLED GRAND HOOSUCK AND LATER SADDLEBACK, THE MOUNTAIN WAS A MAJOR DRAW FOR LITERARY TYPES IN THE LATE 1800S, ATTRACTING THE LIKES OF HERMAN MELVILLE, HENRY DAVID THOREAU, AND NATHANIEL HAW-THORNE. THE IRON WEATHER OBSERVATION TOWER IN THIS VIEW WAS BUILT IN 1885 TO REPLACE ONE CONSTRUCTED IN 1841. NOW, A NINETY-TWO-FOOT GRANITE VETERANS' MEMORIAL, REPORTED TO HAVE BEEN DESIGNED ORIGINALLY AS A LIGHTHOUSE FOR THE CHARLES RIVER IN BOSTON, SITS IN ITS PLACE. THE SUMMIT HOUSE, SHOWN ON THE CARD, WAS SUPPLANTED IN 1937 BY BASCOM LODGE, A STONE HOUSE BUILT BY THE CIVILIAN CONSERVATION CORPS.

The Highest Point in Mass. Summit House and Tower on Greylock Mt.

40. MOUNT WACHUSETT'S FIRST STRUCTURE WAS A SMALL STONE HUT CONSTRUCTED IN 1870. A FEW YEARS LATER A ROAD WAS BUILT TO THE 2,006-FOOT SUMMIT. THE HUT WAS EXPANDED AND A BOWLING ALLEY BUILT. THE FIRST HOTEL WAS OPENED AT THE SUMMIT IN 1882. IT WAS REPLACED IN 1907 BY A "MODERN" STRUCTURE THAT FEATURED RUNNING WATER AND ELECTRICITY. THAT BUILDING BURNED DOWN IN 1970. MOUNT WACHUSETT WAS CLIMBED BY HENRY DAVID THOREAU AND MENTIONED IN A JOHN GREENLEAF WHITTIER POEM. TODAY, MOUNT WACHUSETT IS KNOWN FOR ITS OLD-GROWTH FOREST AND A SKI AREA BEGUN BY THE CIVILIAN CONSERVATION CORPS IN 1930. IN FALL, THOUSANDS OF MIGRATING HAWKS CAN BE SEEN PASSING OVER THE MOUNTAIN IN A SINGLE DAY.

Tiprop House Mt. Wachuset, Mass.

41. Roughly following the route of an ancient Native American footpath, the Mohawk Trail stretches some sixty-two miles from Petersburg Pass on the Massachusetts–New York border east to the Connecticut River at Millers Falls (now Turners Falls). The fortunes of the Mohawk Trail rose with the country's embrace of the automobile and tourism. The trail, which is now a section of Route 2 in Massachusetts, brings motorists past many parks and historic attractions, including North America's only water-carved natural bridge and the site of Fort Massachusetts (built in 1745), both in North Adams. In 1914 the Massachusetts legislature declared the Mohawk Trail a scenic road, the first in the United States. The hairpin turn was, and still is, one of the more popular spots along the fabled drive.

HAIRPIN TURN, MOHAWK TRAIL, MASS.

42. STILL SPORTING TOURIST ACCOMMODATIONS, WHITCOMB SUMMIT, AT 2,272 FEET ABOVE SEA LEVEL, IS THE HIGHEST POINT ON THE SIXTY-TWO-MILE-LONG MOHAWK TRAIL. IT WAS HERE, IN THE TOWN OF FLORIDA, IN OCTOBER 1914 THAT THE ROUTE WAS OFFICIALLY DEDICATED. MORE THAN 1,800 PEOPLE, WHO ARRIVED IN SOME THREE HUNDRED AUTOMOBILES, PARTICI-PATED. PRIVATE BUSINESSES AT THE SUMMIT DURING THE ROUTE'S HEYDAY INCLUDED A MOTEL, GIFT SHOP, RESTAURANT, BAR, AND SNACK BAR. THE TOURIST CABINS BUILT ON WHITCOMB SUMMIT WERE REPORTED TO BE THE FIRST IN NEW ENGLAND. ATOP THE HOOSAC RANGE, THE MOHAWK TRAIL RUNS MORE THAN 1,200 FEET ABOVE THE INFAMOUS HOOSAC TUNNEL.

MOHAWK TRAIL, WHITCOMB SUMMIT, THE TOURISTS' MECCA.

43. At just over 25,000 feet (4.75 miles) in length, the Hoosac Tunnel was the longest in the world when it was completed in 1875. Work on the bore, which was originally conceived as a canal passageway, began in 1851. Workers struggled for ten years with hand drills and gunpowder until the arrival of steam drills and nitroglycerine in 1861. The Hoosac has been called "The Bloody Pit," because 195 lives were lost during construction. The last passenger train traveled through the tunnel in 1958. Today, freight trains owned by Guilford Transportation use the tunnel infrequently.

44. At nearly 400 acres, Mountain Park, at the base of 1,200-foot Mount Tom, near Holyoke, was once considered the largest "street railway park" in the world. It opened in 1895. Trolleys brought patrons from nearby towns to a transfer station, and from there an inclined railway took them to the top of the mountain, where a succession of grand summit hotels were built. Most of the structures were destroyed by fire; the last, long fallen into neglect, was torn down in 1938. Mountain Park sported a zoo, restaurants, a merry-go-round, and a nongambling entertainment "casino" that could seat 2,500 people. Eventually the trolleys stopped and the inclined railway broke down and was abandoned in 1938. Mountain Park continued to operate until 1987.

Mountain Park,
Mt. Tom, Mass.

A 505

45. THE WATERS OF BASH-BISH FALLS, CONSIDERED TO BE THE TALLEST WATERFALL IN SOUTHERN NEW ENGLAND, TUMBLE THROUGH A DEEP GORGE BEFORE BEING SPLIT BY A MASSIVE BOULDER FOR THE EIGHTY-FOOT PLUNGE TO A DARK GREEN POOL BELOW. ONCE PRIVATELY OWNED, THE FALLS ARE NOW CONTROLLED BY THE MASSACHUSETTS PARKS DEPARTMENT AS PART OF THE MOUNT WASHINGTON STATE FOREST. LEGEND HOLDS THAT THE FALLS WERE NAMED FOR A BEAUTIFUL INDIAN MAIDEN, BASH BISH, WHO WAS SENTENCED TO DIE BY BEING SENT OVER THE FALLS IN A CANOE.

BASH-BISH FALLS, NEAR GREAT BARRINGTON, MASS. 13

53379

46. THE LAKE WITH THE LONGEST NAME IN THE UNITED STATES IS KNOWN BY THE LOCALS SIMPLY AS WEBSTER LAKE. THE NATIVE AMERICAN NAME OF THE LAKE, WHICH IS ACTUALLY THREE LAKES CONNECTED BY NARROW CHANNELS, MEANS "THE BOUNDARY FISHING PLACE."

BEACON PARK WAS BEGUN IN 1874 BY A MINISTER WHO BUILT A DANCE PAVILION THERE. THE PARK GREW OVER THE YEARS TO BECOME A MAJOR AMUSEMENT CENTER AND JUMPING-OFF PLACE FOR TROLLEY RIDERS FROM WORCESTER TO ACCESS THE LAKE'S FLEET OF SMALL STEAMBOATS. IT EVENTUALLY INCLUDED A RUSTIC THEATER AND A CAROUSEL IN ADDITION TO THE DANCE PAVILION. IN 1907 A FIRE OF UNKNOWN ORIGIN LEVELED THE BOATHOUSE AND DESTROYED FOUR VESSELS. THE PARK CLOSED IN 1934; IT WAS SOLD IN 1937 AND TURNED INTO A PRIVATE ESTATE.

BOAT LANDING, BEACON PARK.

LAKE CHARGOGGAGOGGMANCHAUGAGOGGCHAUBUNAGUNGAMAUGG, WEBSTER, MASS.

47. CAMEL'S HUMP seems to be a Victorian adaptation of an influential mapmaker's decision to call this distinctive double-humped 4,083-foot mountain "Camel's Rump." Early French explorers called it the Sleeping Lion (sometimes translated as Crouching Lion). It is the third-highest peak in the state and the only major mountain without a ski area or television antenna on top. Vermont's Long Trail, the country's oldest long-distance footpath, crosses Camel's Hump in its 270-mile trip from Massachusetts to Canada. The venerable Green Mountain Club cares for the trail. For more than a hundred miles, the Long Trail shares its route with the Appalachian Trail.

THE ROCKY SUMMIT OF CAMELS HUMP OR CROUCHING LION, GREEN MTS., VT.   55

12-821

48. DESPITE BARRE'S REPUTATION FOR QUARRIED STONE, IT WAS BRICK, WITH GRANITE ACCENTS, THAT WAS THE MATERIAL OF CHOICE WHEN THE TOWN BUILT THIS FIRE STATION ON NORTH MAIN STREET IN 1904. IT IS AN IDENTICAL TWIN TO ONE BUILT AROUND THE SAME TIME IN QUINCY, MASSACHUSETTS. FOUR LOCAL HOSE COMPANIES WERE CONSOLIDATED, AND THE TOWN HIRED ITS FIRST PAID FIREMEN SHORTLY AFTER THE BUILDING (STILL IN USE TODAY) WAS OPENED. HORSE-DRAWN ENGINES REPLACED WAGONS PULLED BY HAND IN 1906. THE TOWN PURCHASED ITS FIRST MOTORIZED FIRE TRUCK IN 1912. ACCORDING TO FIRE CHIEF PETER JOHN, ONE OF THE TEAMS OF HORSES PICTURED ON THIS CARD WAS NAMED TOM AND JERRY.

Fire station,
Barre, Vt.

49. VERMONT'S HIGHEST PEAK, MOUNT MANSFIELD, LOOMS AT 4,393 FEET ABOVE THE TOWN OF STOWE. NAMED FOR A TOWN THAT NO LONGER EXISTS, MOUNT MANSFIELD WAS FORMERLY CALLED *MOZE-O-DE-BE-WADSO* ("MOUNTAIN WITH HEAD LIKE A MOOSE") BY THE ABENAKI INDIANS. EUROPEAN SETTLERS BELIEVED THAT THE MOUNTAIN'S PROFILE, FROM THE EAST, LOOKED LIKE A MAN'S FOREHEAD, NOSE, CHIN, LIPS, AND ADAM'S APPLE. VERMONT'S LONG TRAIL CROSSES THE SUMMIT, INCLUDING ONE SECTION THAT SPORTS AN AREA OF RARE ALPINE VEGETATION. THE SUMMIT HOUSE WAS OPENED IN 1858; IT CLOSED IN 1957 AND WAS LATER TORN DOWN. THE SKI AREA ON MOUNT MANSFIELD GOT ITS START IN 1933 WHEN THE CIVILIAN CONSERVATION CORPS CUT THE FIRST SKI TRAIL, BUT LONG BEFORE THE SKI AREA OPENED NATHANIEL GOODRICH HAD BECOME THE FIRST PERSON TO SKI DOWN THIS MOUNTAIN, IN 1914.

The Nose and Chin of Mt. Mansfield Vt. From the west side

50. With thousand-foot cliffs towering on each side, Smuggler's Notch, near the famed ski resort of Stowe, first earned its name when the widely unpopular Embargo Act of 1807, which prohibited any trade with Britain through U.S. ports, was expanded the following year to also prevent inland trade with Canada. Hard-pressed Vermonters carried goods and herded cattle through the notch to avoid government agents. Later in that century, escaped slaves found safe passage here. During Prohibition, the notch was a favorite route for liquor smugglers. Route 108, which winds its way through the narrow passage, is closed in the winter months. Besides the Hunter and His Dog, pictured on this card, other distinctive rock formations in the notch include Elephant's Head and Singing Bird.

HUNTER AND HIS DOG 75

SMUGGLERS NOTCH IN THE GREEN MTS. OF VERMONT

1A965

51. New England's largest lake, Lake Champlain, is named for the French explorer Samuel de Champlain, who visited the area in 1608. The lake, 120 miles long and up to 12 miles wide, was the birthplace of the American navy during the Revolution in 1776 when Colonel Benedict Arnold's ragtag flotilla delayed a British invasion fleet. The lake is also reported to be home to a Loch Ness—type of creature dubbed "Champ" or "Champy." The steamer pictured here is actually the *Vermont III* (not the *Vermont*, as noted on the card), built in 1903. It ran passengers and freight between Plattsburgh, New York, and Fort Ticonderoga, and to Burlington, Vermont. It was stripped and sold in 1937.

9842. STR. "VERMONT." LAKE CHAMPLAIN.

52. Although Rudyard Kipling may have been inspired to create the character of Mowgli, the boy raised by wolves in *The Jungle Books*, while living in India, it was in Vermont that the author finally put his character on paper. Kipling and his new bride moved to Brattleboro in 1882 and commissioned New York architect Henry Rutgers Marshall to build them a ninety- by twenty-four-foot shingle-style cottage on eleven acres in the village of Dummerston near Brattleboro. They named the cottage Naulakha, which means "precious jewel." The family remained only four years, leaving in 1896. The home, now owned by the Landmark Trust, is operated as a historic inn.

8—Naulhaka, Former Home of Rudyard Kipling, Brattleboro, Vt.

42471-N

53. BUILT BY PATIENTS AND STAFF ON THE THOUSAND-ACRE GROUNDS OF THE BRATTLEBORO RETREAT, A MENTAL HEALTH FACILITY ESTABLISHED IN 1834, THIS TOWER RISES SIXTY-FIVE FEET ABOVE THE HILLTOP. THE GOTHIC-STYLE TOWER WAS BUILT IN 1887–92 TO COMMEMORATE THE INSTITUTION'S FIFTIETH ANNIVERSARY. IT HAS A BRICK CORE FACED WITH RUBBLE STONE, AND GRANITE TRIM. THE TOWER IS KEPT LOCKED EXCEPT FOR A FEW DESIGNATED VIEWING DAYS EACH YEAR. BRATTLEBORO WAS NAMED FOR COLONEL WILLIAM BRATTLE, JR., AN OFFICER IN THE KING'S MILITIA WHO DIED IN 1776. HE NEVER VISITED THE TOWN THAT BEARS HIS NAME.

M. 53 TOWER IN RETREAT PARK, BRATTLEBORO, VT.

Published by W. R. Goldie.

54. Travelers have sought comfort at taverns and inns on this corner of the village green in Woodstock since 1792. Captain Israel Richardson opened a tavern in that year. Later it became the Eagle Hotel, which was replaced by the Woodstock Inn in 1892. The grand structure shown on the card remained until 1968, when its owner, philanthropist Laurance Rockefeller, determined that it was too decrepit to salvage. He had it torn down and the latest incarnation built on the same spot. Outside of Woodstock is the Suicide Six ski area, which is the site of the first rope tow system in America. *Ladies' Home Journal* once named Woodstock "The Prettiest Village in the USA."

WOODSTOCK, INN.

June 25
1907-
This is
where we
are today
& you can
see from
the marks
which
room we
have. Thanks
for your
letters
Mollie

55. CONSIDERED THE HUB OF VERMONT'S "NORTHEAST KINGDOM," ST. JOHNSBURY IN THE EARLY YEARS WAS NAMED BESSBOROUGH AND LATER DUNMORE. COLONEL ETHAN ALLEN SUGGESTED THE NAME ST. JOHN IN HONOR OF HECTOR ST. JEAN DE CREVECOEUR, A POWERFUL EUROPEAN ALLY OF A YOUNG UNITED STATES. MR. CREVECOEUR SUGGESTED ST. JOHNSBURY TO HELP AVOID DUPLICATION WITH OTHER TOWNS SUCH AS ST. JOHN IN NEW BRUNSWICK. THE VILLAGE IS SUPPOSEDLY THE ONLY TOWN ON EARTH NAMED ST. JOHNSBURY. AMONG ITS NOTABLE NATIVE SONS WAS ROBERT HOLBROOK SMITH, ONE OF THE FOUNDERS OF ALCOHOLICS ANONYMOUS.

St. Johnsbury, Vt. Winter Scene.

This is out in front of the store

56. Ethan Allen was the legendary leader of the Green Mountain Boys, a militia formed to oppose New York's control of the area then known as the Hampshire Grants. Allen epitomized the true spirit of independent Vermonters. He fought against the British and helped Benedict Arnold capture Fort Ticonderoga in nearby New York, resulting in a great number of cannon and munitions falling into rebel hands for the siege of Boston. Allen established a homestead at the mouth of the Winooski River in Burlington near a high cliff that legend held was used by Algonquin Indians as a lookout. Allen, who married twice and had five children, died of a stroke in 1789. He was fifty-one years old. His memorial tower, shown on the card, was dedicated in the late summer of 1905.

57. Once considered the tallest battle monument in the world, this imposing tower in Bennington remains the highest structure in Vermont. Finished in 1889, it honors the sacrifice of those who fought in the Battle of Bennington, even though the battle was actually fought in nearby Walloomsac, in 1777. President Benjamin Harrison presided at dedication ceremonies in 1891. The monument, which stands 306 feet tall, is built of limestone quarried in nearby New York. Three states can be seen from the indoor observation deck. Other monuments on the grounds of the Bennington Battle Monument honor Revolutionary War heroes General John Stark and Seth Warner, commander of the Green Mountain Boys.

Bennington Battle Monument, Bennington, Vt.
307 Ft. 9½ Inches in Height, Base 37 by 37 feet.

404-823

58. FED FROM A SPRING ON NEARBY BALD MOUNTAIN, THIS FOUNTAIN, DESIGNED BY SETH HUNT, REPORTEDLY WAS FOR A TIME THE HIGHEST SINGLE-STREAM FOUNTAIN IN THE WORLD. ALTHOUGH THE CARD NOTES A SPRAY HEIGHT OF 187 FEET, OTHER SOURCES CLAIM IT SPRAYED AS HIGH AS 196 FEET INTO THE AIR. THE SOLDIERS' HOME, NOW CALLED THE VERMONT VETERANS' HOME, WAS MR. HUNT'S BIRTHPLACE. THE FOUNTAIN WAS SHUT OFF IN THE EARLY 1990S IN AN EFFORT TO CONSERVE WATER.

Fountain at Vermont Soldiers' Home, Bennington, Vt.
Throws a Stream 187 Feet High.

59. Long before Ben & Jerry's Ice Cream became Vermont's most famous homegrown export, maple syrup grabbed all the taste bud attention. Native Americans called maple sugar *SINZIBUKWUD*, which means "sweet buds." It takes sugar maple trees about forty years to attain the twelve-inch diameter needed for tapping. During sugar time, around the end of February or early March, taps go into the trees. Each tap produces about ten gallons of sap. That ten gallons is boiled down to a quart of syrup. Many producers now use plastic piping to collect sap instead of the traditional metal buckets. Vermont is the nation's largest maple syrup producer; in 2004, some 500,000 gallons were produced. The New England Maple Museum is located on Route 7, just north of Rutland.

"Photo Copyright by L.F. Brehmer." Ye Ancient way of Maple Sugar Making in Vermont.

60. VERMONT HAS LITERALLY HUNDREDS OF NAMED WATERFALLS, SUCH AS THE 88-FOOT "GREAT FALLS OF THE STEVENS RIVER" IN BARNET. UNFORTUNATELY THE DRAMA OF THIS CASCADE IS NOW GONE. THE COVERED BRIDGE WAS REPLACED LONG AGO; A MODERN CONCRETE ABUTMENT FOR A BRIDGE CARRYING ROUTE 5 RESTS WHERE THIS MAN IS STANDING. ACTUALLY, THE MAN WAS MOST LIKELY ADDED BY THE PRINTER AND WAS NOT ATOP THIS DANGEROUS PERCH WHEN THE PHOTO WAS TAKEN. THE POOL AT THE BOTTOM IS ACTUALLY AN IMPOUNDMENT BEHIND A FORMER DAM OWNED BY THE BARNET LIGHT AND POWER STATION. MANY MILLS, INCLUDING THOSE THAT MADE APPLE CIDER AND WOOD PRODUCTS, ONCE LINED THE STEVENS RIVER, WHICH JOINS THE CONNECTICUT RIVER AT BARNET.

Falls on Stevens River, Barnet, Vt.

61. BUILT OF NATIVE TRAPROCK, A TYPE OF VOLCANIC BEDROCK, CASTLE CRAIG ADORNS WEST PEAK, HIGH ABOVE HUBBARD PARK IN MERIDEN. THE THIRTY-THREE-FOOT-TALL TOWER, BUILT IN 1900, WAS A GIFT FROM THE PARK'S NAMESAKE, WALTER HUBBARD, OF BRADLEY AND HUBBARD MANUFACTURING FAME. THE PARK WAS DESIGNED BY THE SONS OF FREDERICK LAW OLMSTED. LOCAL LEGEND TELLS OF A BLACK DOG THAT ROAMS THE NEARBY RIDGES AND FORESTS. IT IS ALWAYS SEEN THREE TIMES: THE FIRST TIME, A VIEWER WILL SOON ENJOY AN INCREASE IN MATERIAL POSSESSIONS; THE SECOND TIME, PHYSICAL AILMENTS WILL BEGIN; THE THIRD TIME, DEATH IS NEAR.

COLLECTION OF CARL BRECHLIN

22. Castle Craig, Hubbard Park. Meriden, Conn.

62. This pile of broken rocks atop West Peak near New Haven is famous as Judges Cave—the hiding place of two English judges who ordered the execution of King Charles I in 1649. When the king's son, Charles II, came to power seeking revenge in 1660, Judges William Goffe and Edward Whalley fled to the colonies. They hid in Boston, Cambridge, and later New Haven before fleeing to the shelter of openings beneath the boulders in the early summer of 1661, when the king's men came to town. Supposedly, during their month-long stay, the men were visited one night by a panther but suffered no harm. Sympathetic settlers nearby left food for the men on a stump and often let them stay in their homes on rainy evenings.

2952—*Judges Cave, West Rock Park, New Haven, Conn.*

James is here come over.

Souvenir Post Card Co., New York and Berlin.

63. NEW HAVEN JOINED SCORES OF TOWNS IN CONNECTI-
CUT IN HONORING CIVIL WAR AND OTHER VETERANS DURING
A SPURT OF MONUMENT BUILDING IN THE 1880S. THE 110-
FOOT-TALL GRANITE PILLAR WITH A BRONZE "ANGEL OF
PEACE," PICTURED ON THIS CARD, WAS BEGUN IN 1886 AND
FINISHED EXACTLY A YEAR LATER. AT THE DEDICATION ON
JUNE 17, 1887, MORE THAN 150,000 PEOPLE WATCHED
20,000 MARCHERS IN A PARADE, IN THE RAIN. AMONG THE
SPEAKERS WERE UNION GENERALS WILLIAM TECUMSEH
SHERMAN AND PHILIP HENRY SHERIDAN. IN ADDITION TO
ITS SACRIFICE IN WAR, NEW HAVEN IS THE HOME OF YALE
UNIVERSITY, AND THE FIRST LOLLIPOP, INVENTED BY
GEORGE C. SMITH IN 1892.

2950—East Rock and Soldiers' Monument looking from Indian Head, New Haven, Conn.

64. Lake Compounce was named for Native American chief John Compound, who sold the lake and nearby land to a settler in 1684. An amusement park on the site began to prosper in the late 1800s and is considered to be the oldest in the United States. Yes, Lovers' Rock is still there. Currently, visitors to the Lake Compounce Theme Park get up close and personal with the rock as they pass by in eight-passenger rafts on the Thunder Rapids Raft Ride. Lovers' Rock currently serves as the base for a waterfall that slashes onto the rafts below. Legend holds that Chief Compound drowned while trying to paddle across the lake in a large brass kettle.

Lovers Rock
Lake Compounce Conn.

65. NOW OFFICIALLY A NATIONAL RECREATIONAL TRAIL, THE THREE-AND-A-HALF-MILE CLIFF WALK IN NEWPORT HAS BEEN POPULAR SINCE 1880. IT FOLLOWS A PUBLIC RIGHT-OF-WAY ACROSS PRIVATE PROPERTY. THROUGHOUT THE YEARS SOME PROPERTY OWNERS HAVE RESISTED PUBLIC ACCESS, EVEN USING DOGS AND BULLS TO INTIMIDATE WALKERS. CLAUS VON BÜLOW WAS A FORMER CLIFF WALK COMMITTEE CHAIRMAN. ALONG THE PATH IS THE SEVENTY-ROOM MANSION THE BREAKERS, BUILT IN 1895 BY CORNELIUS VANDERBILT. VISITED BY MORE THAN 400,000 PEOPLE ANNUALLY, THE BREAKERS IS NOW CARED FOR BY THE PRESERVATION SOCIETY OF NEWPORT COUNTY.

NEWPORT, R.I. The Cliff Walk from "The Breakers."

66. CONSIDERED TO BE THE BIRTHPLACE OF THE INDUSTRIAL REVOLUTION IN EARLY NORTH AMERICA, SLATER'S MILL, ON THE BLACKSTONE RIVER, WAS THE FIRST COTTON MILL IN THE UNITED STATES. SAMUEL SLATER AND PARTNERS BUILT THE WATER-POWERED MILL IN 1793. THE WATER WHEEL POW-ERED A SHAFT THAT TRANSFERRED POWER VIA BELTS TO INDIVIDUAL MACHINES. WITHIN THREE YEARS THERE WERE THIRTY PEOPLE WORKING THERE, MOST OF THEM CHILDREN. THE MILL IS NOW OPEN AS THE OLD SLATER MILL MUSEUM IN PAWTUCKET AND IS PART OF THE BLACKSTONE RIVER VALLEY NATIONAL HERITAGE CORRIDOR, WHICH SPOTLIGHTS DOZENS OF EARLY INDUSTRIAL SITES IN THE AREA.

OLD SLATER MILL, PAWTUCKET, R. I.
FIRST COTTON MILL IN AMERICA.

thanks for Mary pretty card it is just
the card I have liked to get for a long time
Cornelia Storm N.Y. 904. a-113.

67. Like many of New England's early amusement parks, Vanity Fair, in East Providence, had a short but intense life. George B. Boyden created this park in 1907. Riders on Shoot the Chutes, pictured on this card, sat in square-front barges for the quick trip down the ramp into a 1.6-million-gallon pool. Most of the park was destroyed by fire in 1912. An oil tank farm and a small golf course now occupy the site.

9113   THE CHUTE, THE CHUTES, VANITY FAIR, R. I.

68. As is frequently the case with old postcards, the actual location of a site may differ from the town listed on the card. Cobble Rock is such a case. Early card merchants chose names of nearby towns they felt would help boost sales. Cobble Rock, which became famous for having the names of visitors carved into or painted on it, is actually located in North Smithfield. The boulder dislodged and rolled over during a thunderstorm in the fall of 1977. Today it rests in woods on private property.

COBBLE ROCK, WOONSOCKET, R. I.

69. WHITE MOUNTAIN GUIDE, TRAPPER, HUNTER, AND SOMETIMES HERMIT JAMES "JACK" ALLEN WAS BORN IN SEBEC, MAINE, IN 1835. A CIVIL WAR VETERAN, HE SPENT THE LAST FORTY YEARS OF HIS LIFE IN THE ALBANY INTERVALE IN NEW HAMPSHIRE. DESCRIBED AS A BLUFF, HEARTY, JOVIAL, FUN-LOVING FELLOW, HE HELD SEVERAL WOODS-RELATED JOBS AND LIVED FOR A TIME IN THIS RUSTIC CABIN ON BEAR MOUNTAIN. HE DIED IN JULY 1912.

Old Jack of the Mountain, White Mountains, N.H.

70. THIS IRON TOWER, ATOP 2,394-FOOT MOUNT AGASSIZ, OUTSIDE BETHLEHEM, NEW HAMPSHIRE, WENT INTO SERVICE IN 1910 AS ONE OF THE FIRST FOREST FIRE LOOKOUT TOWERS IN NEW ENGLAND. THE PEAK BOASTS EXPANSIVE VIEWS OF THE SURROUNDING RANGES, INCLUDING THE PERCY PEAKS, FRANCONIA MOUNTAINS, AND PRESIDENTIAL RANGE. THE MOUNTAIN IS NAMED AFTER LOUIS AGASSIZ, A NATURAL-HISTORY PROFESSOR WHO DEVELOPED HIS BREAK-THROUGH THEORY ON GLACIATION AS A PRIMARY AGENT OF GEOLOGIC CHANGE AFTER SEEING SCRATCHES ON THE PEAK. BETHLEHEM, WHICH POSTMARKS TENS OF THOUSANDS OF CHRISTMAS CARDS EACH YEAR, IS THE HIGHEST TOWN IN NEW ENGLAND, AT 1,450 FEET ABOVE SEA LEVEL.

Bethlehem, N. H.   Top of Mt. Agassiz.

71. New Hampshire's mountains have some of the worst weather in the world, as the builders of the Peak House, atop 3,475-foot Mount Chocorua, discovered in the fall of 1915. On September 26, wild winds ripped apart the sturdy timber building. Luckily, no one was inside. In 1924 a cabin was built on the site. Its roof was blown off in 1932. Its replacement, the Jim Liberty Cabin which still stands, had chains installed to keep the roof intact. Chocorua was named after a Sokosis Indian chief who reportedly died on the mountain in the early 1700s. Some legends say he fell, others that he was shot by settlers.

MT. CHOCORUA AND PEAK HOUSE, WHITE MTS., N.H.

72. New Hampshire is full of places touting unique rock formations that look like lions, ducks, elephants, or famous presidents. In Thorn Mountain Park in Jackson, the Washington Boulder, which looks out on Mount Washington, is one of the most famous of these formations. A ski area once operated on the site. Many viewers see the profile of America's first president; some think the formation looks more like Alfred Hitchcock.

THE WASHINGTON BOULDER. THORN MOUNTAIN PARK. JACKSON, N. H.

73. WHETHER OR NOT THIS REALLY IS THE LARGEST BOULDER IN THE WORLD REMAINS A SUBJECT OF SOME DEBATE. WHAT IS CERTAIN, HOWEVER, IS THAT THE MAZE OF TUNNELS AND CHAMBERS AT THE BASE OF HAWK'S CLIFF ON MOUNT HAYCOCK, IN PLYMOUTH, IS WORTH SEEING. VISITORS TO THE POLAR CAVES PARK, WHICH OPENED IN 1922, DESCEND AS MUCH AS 20 FEET AND CAN SCRAMBLE AMONG MASSIVE BOULDERS BROKEN FROM THE CLIFF BY THE LAST GLACIER MORE THAN 50,000 YEARS AGO. THE AIR IN THE CAVES IS COOL ALL SUMMER LONG.

VIEW FROM TOP OF WORLD'S LARGEST BOULDER, POLAR CAVES, N. H.

3630

74. THE FIRST STEAMBOAT ON TEN-MILE-LONG LAKE SUNAPEE WAS THE 47-FOOT *LADY WOODSUM*, LAUNCHED IN 1875. SOON OTHERS JOINED THE FLEET OPERATED BY THE WOODSUM BROTHERS, INCLUDING THE *KEARSARGE* (AT LEFT) AND THE *ARMENIA* (AT RIGHT), THE COMPANY'S FLAGSHIP. THE STEAMERS MET TRAINS AND TRANSFERRED PASSENGERS AT LAKE STATION AT NEWBURY HARBOR, AT THE LAKE'S SOUTHERN END, AND SUNAPEE HARBOR, FARTHER UP THE LAKE. *SUNAPEE* IS REPORTEDLY THE ALGONQUIN WORD FOR "WILD GOOSE LAKE."

STEAMERS AT LAKE STATION, LAKE SUNAPEE, N.H.

75. Lake Sunapee boasts three lighthouses, all built in the early 1890s by the Woodsum brothers, owners of the steamboat line serving the lake. The Loon Island light was the first, built in 1891 after the steamer *Edmond Burke* wrecked on the rocky outcrop near the middle of the lake. The twenty-five-foot tower was hit by lightning and burned flat in 1960. It was rebuilt later that summer, and was converted to solar power in 1980. The Lake Sunapee Protective Association now maintains all three lighthouses.

Light House and Sunapee Mt., Lake Sunapee, N. H.

76. WITH AS MANY AS 125,000 PEOPLE HIKING TO THE
TOP ANNUALLY, MOUNT MONADNOCK, NEAR JAFFREY, IS
CONSIDERED BY SOME TO BE THE MOST-CLIMBED MOUNTAIN
IN THE WORLD. NEW ENGLANDERS SAY THAT MOUNT MONAD-
NOCK TOOK THAT TITLE AWAY FROM JAPAN'S MOUNT FUJI
AFTER PUBLIC TRANSIT ACCESS OPENED ON FUJIYAMA IN
1991. THE 3,166-FOOT MONADNOCK HAS ATTRACTED THE
LIKES OF HENRY DAVID THOREAU AND RALPH WALDO EMER-
SON AND WAS FIRST CLIMBED IN 1725. THE PEAK WAS
ONCE ENTIRELY FORESTED, BUT YEARS OF FIRES, CUTTING,
AND OTHER INSULTS AT THE HAND OF MAN HAVE LEFT THE
TOP OPEN AND BARREN. THE FOUNDATIONS OF THE "RAIN
SHELTER" REMAIN NEAR THE MOUNTAIN'S SUMMIT.

Published by Duncan, The Druggist   The Rain Shelter, Monadnock Mt., Jaffrey, N. H.

77. The Uncanoonuc Incline Railway opened in 1907 to bring sightseers and summit hotel guests to the top of 1,321-foot Uncanoonuc Mountain. Native Americans had reportedly named the twin peaks after women's breasts. Riders took a trolley from Shirley Junction to the base station, then transferred to the incline railway. It took about five minutes for the electric cars to lumber up the 35 percent grade to the top. In the 1930s the mission of the incline railway changed from ferrying summer visitors to carrying skiers. The incline kept running until 1941, when a fire damaged a long section of track. The remaining infrastructure was then torn down.

BASE OF UNCANOONUC MOUNTAIN, SHOWING INCLINE RAILWAY, MANCHESTER, N. H.

78. This forty-foot tower on the end of Spindle Point is actually located in the village of Meredith, not Weirs as noted on the card. Built in 1892 by Colonel Charles Cummings, it served as a lighthouse and is still standing on the shore of 72-square-mile Lake Winnipesaukee. The village of Weirs, which is part of Laconia, is named for the fish-snaring device used by Native Americans at the outlet of the lake. Laconia and Weirs Beach is the epicenter for the annual Bike Week, which in 2003 drew an estimated 350,000 motor-cyclists to the area. Officials estimate they spent more than $240 million dollars while visiting.

LAKE WINNIPESAUKEE, N.H., SPINDLE POINT OBSERVATORY, WEIRS.

79. THE GRANDEST OF ALL LAKE WINNIPESAUKEE'S STEAMERS, THE 178-FOOT *MOUNT WASHINGTON* WAS LAUNCHED AT ALTON BAY IN 1872. WITH A SINGLE FORTY-TWO-INCH PISTON, SHE COULD STEAM AT A BREAKNECK TWENTY-FIVE KNOTS, EASILY OUTPACING HER OLDER RIVAL *THE LADY OF THE LAKE*, WHICH BEGAN SERVICE IN 1849 AND CONTINUED UNTIL 1893. THE *MOUNT WASHINGTON* CARRIED PASSENGERS AND CARGO TO ALL THE VILLAGES AND ISLANDS AROUND THE LAKE UNTIL DECEMBER 1939, WHEN SHE WAS DESTROYED IN A FIRE THAT LEVELED THE RAILROAD STATION AND DOCK AT WEIRS. THE *MOUNT WASHINGTON II* WAS LAUNCHED A YEAR LATER AND CONTINUES TODAY IN EXCURSION SERVICE.

Lake Winnipesaukee, N.H. Str. "Mt. Washington" Arriving at Wharf, Centre Harbor.

65198

80. Between 1885 and 1910 there were more than two hundred hotels, inns, and boardinghouses in the Mount Washington area. Among the first was Colonel Joseph Thompson's Glen House, built in Pinkham Notch, on the eastern side of Mount Washington, in 1852. The establishment went through several incarnations and renovations before the last one was destroyed by fire in 1967. The Glen House was located at the beginning of the Mount Washington carriage road, which is still used by automobiles. On this card, passengers atop the Tally-Ho stage are headed to the railroad station a few miles away at Glen Station, just above North Conway.

White Mts. N.H.
The Tally-Ho leaving the Glen House for Glen Station

81. MARSHFIELD STATION, AT THE BASE OF THE MOUNT WASHINGTON COG RAILWAY, WAS NAMED FOR SYLVESTER MARSH, BACKER OF THE TOURIST LINE, AND DARBY FIELD, THE FIRST EUROPEAN TO CLIMB TO THE TOP OF NEW ENGLAND'S HIGHEST MOUNTAIN, IN 1642. THE SMALL BUILDING AT THE CENTER OF THE CARD IS STILL IN USE TODAY. SEVERAL RAILROAD TRACKS CONVERGED AT THE NEARBY FABYAN HOUSE, AND A SPUR RAN DIRECTLY TO THE BASE STATION. IN 1932, AFTER AN AUTO ROAD WAS BUILT TO MARSHFIELD STATION, THE RAIL SPUR WAS TORN UP. THE FABYAN HOUSE BURNED DOWN IN 1951.

At the Base of Mt. Washington Station.

82. WORK ON A DARING ROAD TO THE SUMMIT OF MOUNT WASHINGTON BEGAN IN 1854. AFTER REACHING THE HALFWAY MARK, THE FIRST COMPANY WENT BANKRUPT. THE EIGHT-MILE-LONG CARRIAGE ROAD, WHICH ASCENDS A VERTICAL MILE, WAS FINALLY OPENED ON AUGUST 8, 1861. THE GLEN HOUSE (SEE POSTCARD 80) STABLED MORE THAN A HUNDRED HORSES NEEDED TO TAKE TURNS PULLING WAGONLOADS OF TOURISTS TO THE TOP OF THE MOUNTAIN. MR. AND MRS. FREELAN STANLEY MADE THE FIRST POWERED ASCENT IN THEIR STEAM-DRIVEN LOCOMOBILE IN AUGUST 1899. THE NAME OF THE ROAD WAS OFFICIALLY CHANGED FROM "CARRIAGE ROAD" TO "AUTO ROAD" IN 1911. VISITORS STILL RIDE TO THE SUMMIT IN "STAGECOACHES" (VANS). THOSE WHO PAY THE TOLL TO TAKE A PRIVATE VEHICLE TO THE TOP GET A BUMPER STICKER BOASTING, "THIS CAR CLIMBED MT. WASHINGTON."

Toll Houses, Base Mt. Washington Carriage Road, N.H.

83. Built almost entirely on a 3.1-mile-long trestle, the Mount Washington Cog Railway made its first run to the 6,288-foot summit on July 3, 1869. The steam locomotives employ a stout cog that engages a rack that runs up the center of the line; there is not enough friction for conventional wheeled power. On Jacob's Ladder, a twenty-five-foot-high span, the rails have a gradient of nearly 37 percent, making the line the second-steepest railroad in the world. (The steepest is in Switzerland.) On a typical run, a locomotive burns about a ton of coal and uses about a thousand gallons of water. Passengers in the open-air cars enjoy spectacular views as well as billows of smoke and steam.

Jacob's Ladder. Mt. Washington Ry.

Greetings from Mt. Washington.

Published by Chisholm Bros., Portland, Me.   Nº73.   MADE IN GERMANY.

From
Uncle Will

84. Named for Edward Tuckerman, a botanist who explored the White Mountains during the 1800s, Tuckerman's Ravine, on the east side of Mount Washington, features snow that is skiable well into June. This high glacial cirque was first skied in 1926. Racing began soon after. The record for the Inferno Race from the summit to the Appalachian Mountain Club hut at the bottom was set by a 19-year-old Austrian named Toni Matt in 1939. The elevation drop is 4,200 feet over four miles, including a plunge over the near-vertical 800-foot head wall. Matt did it in just six minutes and twenty-nine seconds. Today, despite the risks of avalanche and falls that have claimed many lives, thousands of skiers and snowboarders trudge into Tuckerman's each spring to test their skill.

TUCKERMAN'S RAVINE, MT. WASHINGTON, WHITE MTS., N. H.

85. Called "the home of the world's worst weather," Mount Washington lies in the major storm track on the eastern seaboard. Winds exceeding seventy-five miles per hour (hurricane force) are recorded on more than a hundred days each year. Clouds obscure the summit for at least part of the day on three hundred days annually. An average year has 256 inches of snow. Weather observations were made from the summit from 1870 to 1892 and have been done continuously since 1932. On April 12, 1934, the highest surface wind gust ever recorded on Earth, 231 miles per hour, was logged at the summit. That same year, in January, the record for cold was reached at −47 degrees Fahrenheit. It has never been warmer than 72 degrees Fahrenheit on top.

White Mts. N.H., Mt. Washington. Above the Clouds.

86. The Tip Top House was built on the summit of Mount Washington in 1853 on the heels of the success of the Summit House, built the previous year. Located right near the geographical summit, the Tip Top House had walls built of stone blasted from the mountain itself. The first version had a flat roof. A pitched roof replaced it in the 1860s, and chains were thrown across the roof to help the 24- by 84-foot building withstand high winds. In 1877 a newspaper called *Among the Clouds* began publishing from the building. The structure was destroyed by fire in 1908; it took only eleven days to rebuild it. Like the Summit House, the fortunes of the Tip Top House waxed and waned over the years. It was restored in 1987 and is open to day visitors.

COPR. DETROIT PHOTOGRAPHIC CO.

5517 TIP TOP HOUSE, SUMMIT OF MT. WASHINGTON, WHITE MTS., N. H.

87. LIZZIE BOURNE, TWENTY-THREE, WAS THE SECOND RECORDED DEATH ON MOUNT WASHINGTON; THE FIRST WAS ENGLISHMAN FREDRICK STICKLAND, TWENTY-NINE, IN OCTOBER 1849. LIZZIE PERISHED OF EXHAUSTION AND EXPOSURE NEAR THE SUMMIT DURING A STORM, JUST A FEW YARDS FROM SAFETY, ON SEPTEMBER 14, 1855. THE SPOT WERE SHE LAY, NEAR THE COG RAILWAY TRACK, STILL SPORTS A CRUDE MEMORIAL. OFFICIALS ESTIMATE THAT MORE THAN 130 PEOPLE HAVE DIED IN THE MOUNT WASHINGTON RANGE FROM A VARIETY OF CAUSES INCLUDING FALLS, EXPOSURE, HEART ATTACKS, AND AUTO OR COG RAILWAY ACCIDENTS. THE FATALITY RATE HAS EARNED MOUNT WASHINGTON THE MONIKER "THE MOST DANGEROUS SMALL MOUNTAIN IN THE WORLD." MORE PEOPLE HAVE DIED THERE THAN ON ANY OTHER PEAK IN THE COUNTRY.

Published in Germany for G. W. Morris, Portland, Me.

SUMMIT HOUSE FROM LIZZIE BOURNE MONUMENT, MT. WASHINGTON, N. H.

88. CALLED "THE CLUB IN THE CLOUDS," THE MOUNT WASHINGTON CLUB WAS A POPULAR SPOT IN THE SUMMIT HOUSE ATOP MOUNT WASHINGTON FOR SOME SEVENTY YEARS. IN SEASON, VISITORS COULD ENJOY A MEAL, OVERNIGHT ACCOMMODATIONS, AND VIEWS OF MORE THAN A HUNDRED MILES (ON CLEAR DAYS). ALL COG RAILROAD PASSENGERS BECAME AUTOMATIC MEMBERS. THE WOODEN SUMMIT HOUSE, ABANDONED IN 1968, WAS TORN DOWN IN 1978 TO CLEAR THE WAY FOR THE PRESENT SHERMAN ADAMS SUMMIT BUILDING, OWNED BY THE STATE OF NEW HAMPSHIRE.

AT THE TOP OF THE WORLD,
MT. WASHINGTON CLUB.

WHITE MOUNTAINS,
N. H.—313

89. The Presidential Range has long been a hiker's haven, and the system of high huts maintained by the Appalachian Mountain Club (AMC) can claim much of the credit. A bed and meals can be had at most of the huts, including Lonesome Lake (2,760 feet), Greenleaf (4,200 feet), Galehead (3,800 feet), Zealand Falls (2,700 feet), Mizpah Springs (3,800 feet), Lakes of the Clouds (5,050 feet), Madison (4,800 feet), and Carter Notch (3,288 feet). The first shelter was erected in 1901 at Lakes of the Clouds. The present facility, which features some solar and wind power, can sleep ninety people in several coed bunk rooms. Hut staff prepare meals and teach visitors how to fold their blankets the AMC way. Founded in 1876, the AMC is the oldest recreation and conservation group in the country.

White Mts. N.H. Mt Washington, Lake of the Clouds and Crawford Trail from Summit.

90. More than 15,000 years ago, a massive glacier pushed out of the north and carved New Hampshire's distinctive U-shaped valleys, including the renowned Pinkham, Crawford, and Franconia notches. Hunter Timothy Nash, from Lancaster, first described Crawford Notch in 1771. It was later settled by members of the Crawford family.

In Crawford Notch, a major geological calamity befell the Samuel Willey, Jr., family in August 1826. Heavy rains swelled the Saco River in the valley and unleashed a terrible avalanche of mud, dirt, and rocks. Although they had apparently tried to flee to safety, Samuel Willey and his wife, five children, and two hired hands died in the disaster. Ironically, they probably would have survived if they had stayed put, for the avalanche path split and went around the family's house.

White Mts. N.H. Crawford Notch from Mt. Willard.

91. The railroad first pushed through rugged Crawford Notch in 1857. Heading north from North Conway, the line gained 1,623 feet in altitude in just thirty miles. The railroad bridge pictured in the card, over Willey Brook, was 400 feet long and 100 feet high. The other major span on the Maine Central tracks was the Frankenstein Trestle, at 80 feet high and 500 feet long. The building shown on the card is the Mount Willard Section House, which was used to shelter track workers. It could be reached only by rail or on foot. One worker's wife, Hattie Evans, gave birth to four children in the structure. With each new arrival a special train was dispatched to bring a doctor to the family.

THE HEART OF CRAWFORD NOTCH, WHITE MOUNTAINS, N. H.

92. Overlooking the thirty-two-acre spring-fed Lake Gloriette, the stately Balsams is one of New Hampshire's three remaining grand hotels. The Balsams started in 1866 as a modest twenty-five-room boardinghouse called the Dix House. It was named for Colonel Timothy Dix, founder of the town of Dixville Notch. With a change in ownership in 1895, it adopted its current name, and by 1918 it could accommodate up to four hundred guests and had a grand ballroom and numerous other buildings. Today, the Balsams encompasses a twenty-five-square-mile estate that includes its own ski area, tennis courts, golf courses, hiking trails, bike paths, cross-country ski trails, and numerous other attractions.

THE BALSAMS AND LAKE GLORIETTE, DIXVILLE NOTCH, N. H.

93. ALTHOUGH NEW HAMPSHIRE IS MOST FAMOUS FOR THE STONE PROFILE OF THE OLD MAN OF THE MOUNTAIN, THIS SILHOUETTE OF MARTHA WASHINGTON IN TINY (127-ACRE) DIXVILLE STATE PARK ALSO DRAWS PLENTY OF VISITORS. DIXVILLE NOTCH IS BEST KNOWN NATIONALLY FOR ITS "FIRST IN THE NATION" ELECTION RESULTS. SINCE 1960, THE POLLS HAVE OPENED JUST AFTER MIDNIGHT IN THE BALLROOM AT THE BALSAMS. PROVIDED THAT ALL THIRTY OR SO REGISTERED VOTERS ARE PRESENT, BALLOTING IS USUALLY OVER IN A MINUTE AND THE RESULTS ARE RELEASED. SINCE 1968 DIXVILLE HAS CORRECTLY PICKED THE REPUBLICAN PRESIDENTIAL NOMINEE IN PRIMARY BALLOTING.

MARTHA WASHINGTON PROFILE, DIXVILLE NOTCH, WHITE MTS., N. H.

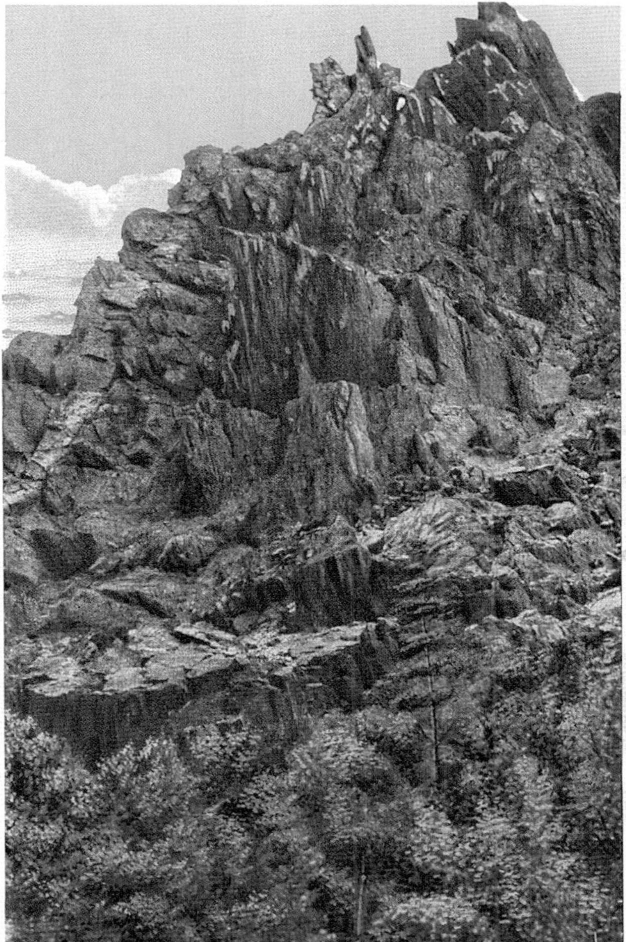

94. Looking more like cowboys than tourists, these visitors to the Bretton Woods resort were actually riding donkeys as they enjoyed a portion of the resort's extensive bridle path network. One of the more popular destinations was the Upper and Lower Falls—more cascades really—on the Ammonoosuc River where it comes off Mount Washington. Especially in the 1800s, most people would not even think of walking to the top of a tall mountain. Many early trails, including the Crawford Path—Mount Washington's first—and the Davis, Thompson, Fabyan, and Edmands trails were used by people on horseback. In addition to young men of stout constitution carrying heavy loads, mules were used to supply the AMC's High Hut System.

51:—Bretton Woods Rangers on Trail Ponies,

White Mts., N. H.

95. The Mount Pleasant was the first large hotel built at Bretton Woods; it was constructed in 1876. Royal governor John Wentworth named the area in 1772 after his ancestral home, Bretton Hall, in Yorkshire, England. In 1902, the Mount Washington Hotel was built nearby in Bretton Woods. As many as fifty-seven trains a day stopped at Bretton Woods station in the town's heyday. In 1944, Bretton Woods was the site of a conference of bankers and financiers from all over the world who gathered to discuss restoring the world's economy after World War II. Among the institutions created after that meeting were the International Monetary Fund and the World Bank. The Mount Pleasant hotel was torn down in 1939. The Mount Washington remains open today.

71252 THE MOUNT PLEASANT, BRETTON WOODS, WHITE MTS., N. H.

96. The White Mountains stand tall behind the Mount Washington Hotel at Bretton Woods. The summits of the Presidential Range, from southwest to northeast, are Mt. Webster (Daniel Webster), Mt. Jackson (Andrew Jackson), Mt. Pierce (Franklin Pierce), Mt. Eisenhower (Dwight Eisenhower), Mt. Franklin (Ben Franklin), Mt. Monroe (James Monroe), Mt. Washington (George Washington), Mt. Clay (Henry Clay), Mt. Jefferson (Thomas Jefferson), Mt. Sam Adams (Samuel Adams), Mt. Adams (John Adams), Mt. Quincy Adams (John Quincy Adams), and Mt. Madison (James Madison). Five of the peaks appear on this card. In 2003 the state legislature voted to rename Mt. Clay in honor of President Reagan. That's fine for state purposes, but it will not appear on national maps until approved by the U.S. Board of Geographic Names.

Mt. Jefferson Mt. Clay Mt. Wash. Ry. Burt Ravine Mt. Washington Ammonoosuc Ravine Lake of the Clouds Mt. Monroe Mt. Franklin

THE PRESIDENTIAL RANGE AND THE MOUNT WASHINGTON, BRETTON WOODS, WHITE MOUNTAINS, N. H.

97. With an opening of only eighteen inches, the Lemon Squeezer, on the path through the Lost River Reservation in North Woodstock, is not for the chubby or claustrophobic. Lost River was discovered by two brothers, Royal and Lyman Jackman, in 1852 after one of them slipped and fell fifteen feet into a cave created by a jumble of boulders at the bottom of Kinsman Notch. The river got its name because it disappears into the pile of boulders. After it reemerges, it drains into the nearby Pemigewasset River.

THE LEMON SQUEEZER, LOST RIVER, WHITE MTS., N. H.   82031

98. HALL OF SHIPS, IN THE LOST RIVER RESERVATION, IS NAMED FOR ROCK FORMATIONS THAT APPEAR TO BE AN OVERTURNED ROWBOAT, THE BOW OF A SHIP, AND THE KEEL OF A SAILBOAT. OTHER NAMED SPOTS ALONG THE PATH INCLUDE THE CAVE OF SILENCE AND GUILLOTINE ROCK. AN INTRICATE SERIES OF STEPS, PLATFORMS, AND BOARDWALKS HELPS EASE VISITORS THROUGH THE RUGGED TERRAIN. THERE ARE BYPASSES AROUND NARROW OR ARDUOUS SECTIONS.

HALL-OF-SHIPS, LOST RIVER, WHITE MOUNTAINS, N. H.

99. ONE OF THE MOST SPECTACULAR NATURAL WONDERS OF THE WHITE MOUNTAINS IS THE FLUME, A GORGE THAT IS 800 FEET LONG, 12 TO 20 FEET WIDE, AND 90 FEET DEEP, CUT THROUGH SOLID ROCK. IT FEATURES SEVERAL MAJOR CASCADES AND A POOL THAT IS 150 FEET ACROSS AND 40 FEET DEEP AND SURROUNDED BY 130-FOOT CLIFFS. THIS SPOT WAS DISCOVERED BY 93-YEAR-OLD AUNT JESS IN 1808 WHILE SHE WAS OUT FISHING. FLUMES ARE A COMMON GEOLOGICAL FEATURE IN NEW HAMP-SHIRE. THEY ARE FORMED WHEN DIKES OF SOFTER ROCK BETWEEN GRANITE LAYERS ARE ERODED AWAY BY FAST-MOVING WATER AND ICE. THE FLUME IS NOW A STATE PARK.

THE FLUME LOOKING UP, WHITE MTS., N. H.

100. NEW HAMPSHIRE'S PROUD SYMBOL—AND, INDEED, AN ICON FOR FLINTY NEW ENGLAND TYPES EVERYWHERE—WAS THE OLD MAN OF THE MOUNTAIN, OVERLOOKING FRANCONIA NOTCH. IT TUMBLED, UNSEEN, FROM THE CLIFF ON MAY 3, 2003. FOR YEARS THE DISTINC-TIVE PROFILE HAD BEEN HELD TOGETHER WITH STEEL CABLES AND EPOXY. A SPECIAL TASK FORCE DECIDED NOT TO REPLACE THE FACE AFTER IT FELL.

DANIEL WEBSTER HAD THIS TO SAY ABOUT THE OLD MAN: "MEN HANG OUT THEIR SIGNS INDICATIVE OF THEIR RESPECTIVE TRADES; SHOEMAKERS HANG OUT A GIGAN-TIC SHOE; JEWELERS A MONSTER WATCH, AND THE DENTIST HANGS OUT A GOLD TOOTH; BUT UP IN THE MOUNTAINS OF NEW HAMP-SHIRE, GOD ALMIGHTY HAS HUNG OUT A SIGN TO SHOW THAT THERE HE MAKES MEN."

Old Man of the Mountain, Franconia Notch,
White Mountains, N. H.

222375

To learn more

MAINE

BETHEL HISTORICAL SOCIETY
10 Broad St. (P.O. Box 12)
Bethel, ME 04217-0012
207-824-2908
www.bethelhistorical.org

BROWNVILLE/BROWNVILLE JUNCTION HISTORICAL SOCIETY
P.O. Box 750
Brownville, ME 04414
207-943-2185 • info at
www.mainemuseums.org

MOOSEHEAD HISTORICAL SOCIETY
P.O. Box 1116
Greenville, Maine 04441-1116
207-695-2909
www.mooseheadhistory.org

PATTEN LUMBERMEN'S MUSEUM
Waters Rd. (P.O. Box 300)
Patten, ME 04765
207-528-2650
lumbermensmuseum.org

RANGELEY LAKES HISTORICAL SOCIETY
Main St. (P.O. Box 521)
Rangeley, ME 04970
207-864-5571

RANGELEY LAKES REGION HISTORICAL SOCIETY
Rte 16, Dead River Rd.
(P.O. Box 740)
Rangeley, ME 04970
207-864-5647 • info at
www.mainemuseums.org

RANGELEY LAKES REGION LOGGING MUSEUM
P.O. Box 154
Rangeley, ME 04970
207-864-3939 • info at
www.mainemuseums.org

RUMFORD AREA HISTORICAL SOCIETY
Municipal Building
Congress Street
Rumford, ME 04276
207-364-4067 • info at
www.mainemuseums.org

MASSACHUSETTS

BERKSHIRE HILLS VISITORS BUREAU
Berkshire Common Plaza
Pittsfield, MA 01201
800-237-5747
www.berkshires.org

MASSACHUSETTS HISTORICAL SOCIETY
1154 Boylston Street
Boston, MA 02215-3695
617-536-1608
www.masshist.org

MOHAWK TRAIL ASSOCIATION
P.O. Box 1044
North Adams, MA 01247
413-743-8127
www.mohawktrail.org

VERMONT

ETHAN ALLEN HOMESTEAD MUSEUM
1 Ethan Allen Homestead
Burlington, VT 05401
802-865-4556
www.ethanallenhomestead.org